The Memory of Light

The Light Poetry Series

Book 1
The Light That Heals

Book 2
A Movement of Light

Book 3
Light in Slow Motion

Book 4
The Memory of Light

The Memory of Light

Keith Wrassmann

AVAILABLE LIGHT PRESS
Maineville, Ohio

Printed in the United States of America.

ISBN: 978-1-961631-05-2
ISBN: 978-1-961631-06-9 (ebook)

Library of Congress Control Number: 2026937578

First Edition

Published by Available Light Press, Maineville, Ohio.

www.availablelightpress.com

Visit the author's website at www.keithwrassmann.com

For life and light
in the forgetting.

Contents

Forgetting is the essence of the thing,
the golden shore a memory that dims
within the guise of self-restricted sight.
But darkness is the pawn of sacred light,
employed to mask the truth that hides within.

The Memory of Light

Discover

Dear Soul,
you become through experience,
whether you perceive it or not.
Life is but a momentary dream
where all you hope for labors to be born,
to show itself as worthy of the pain.
Such sacrifice demands a just reward,
one that brings fulfillment
in the aftermath of the effort.
Give.
Receive.
Long for.
Be fulfilled.
Journey along the path
not knowing where it leads,
for it is here where you discover
all you set aside to find again.
The amnesia of the in-between
is where purpose unfolds,
only to reveal itself fully in the end,
like knowing,
then forgetting,
and then knowing again.

Undiscovered Spaces

Lessons hide in everything,
in every interaction,
planned or unplanned.
This is the way of the world
that never stops giving,
whether your hand is open or closed.
The purpose is not to do,
or to accomplish,
but to perceive through the doing,
for the doing is the action of the moment,
that you may see all it offers.
Success and failure are different perspectives
on the potential of experience.
Purpose is in the gain,
regardless of the outcome.
To live is to move through undiscovered spaces.
To know is the greatest reward.

Masked

Abandonment is the antithesis of love.
The soul whose nature is love
cannot conceive of the possibility
of separation,
for it has only known the one.
So, it embarks on a journey
to embrace illusionary realms
that it may discover itself
in the potential of unbounded darkness.
Forgetting is the essence of the thing,
the golden shore a memory that dims
within the guise of self-restricted sight.
But darkness is the pawn of sacred light,
employed to mask the truth that hides within.
The game of love and loss
is real but for the moment
in the descending,
in the pain it brings,
for the finding out,
for the unfolding of understanding
through experience of all there is to know.

Endings

Fall is turning to winter.
There's nothing you can do.
Soon, the wind will sweep away the leaves
and take them to their final resting place,
where no one can follow or find out.
Once vibrant oranges, yellows, and reds
will fade to all shades of bitter brown.
It's the struggle of endings
in holding on to the beauty of the world—
beauty even in the descent.
You do not want it to end,
for fear is in the ending,
in the disappearance of what you cherished,
in what you knew,
in the uncertainty of location,
in what happens next.
The purpose is in the hiddenness
that you can only accept
by reconciling it as mystery,
so that you may experience
what it is to love and then lose.

Presence

The light was always there,
you just could not see it.
So you struggled with hardship
and loss
until you stopped caring.
Life was no longer about fulfilling desire,
but about getting through each day.
Hope and faith faded to bitterness.
Why does darkness move with such force,
enough to dim light? you asked.
The light replied,
Because it is purposed to show you
what light can only imagine
from its perspective of brilliance.
Darkness must do its work
so you can understand all potential existence.
And so, it did.
Nowhere was life so cruel
than in the illusion of abandonment.
But this descent was only momentary,
for you ascended in a rebirth of majesty.
And the light was always there,
you just could not see it.

Integrate

The experience you fear
is what you do not understand fully,
though you may have tasted it
enough to recognize its nature.
You run from pain
because it hurts in the physical.
But pain is a gateway to expansion.
Threats of discomfort
point you in the right direction,
if what you desire is to know,
to comprehend,
to see the limits of what you lack.
It is not wholeness that you lack,
but the firsthand knowledge of
the infinite potential of experience,
and how you handle fear,
that you may integrate the lessons of living—
the experiences that push you past yourself,
that make you who you are.

Fragment

In the shadow of all that is,
the dimness is a purposed fragmentation.
Scattered light pretends it is unique.
You cannot see the thread
that connects you with those you love
or hate.
You cannot see the place from where you came.
Such is life in the forgetting,
where duality grants the opportunity
of infinite potential,
to be and become,
to lack and to lose.
A moment of peace.
A moment of torment.
But only one moment exists,
protracted into the illusion of time and space,
for the perspective of past and future.
Each soul belongs to the existence of the one,
and from it comes,
and in it lives and moves,
going everywhere and nowhere,
feeling everything and nothing,
all the while standing on the golden shore,
though you know it not.

Living

By the end,
you will have gone farther
than you thought you ever could
when dreaming of such a journey.
This is the default of living,
that each day moves you forward
toward a forgotten destination.
The need for purpose is a distraction
you seek to prove your worth while on the way.
But you do not need to justify your life—
you only need to live.
In living,
you give yourself the right to make mistakes,
to find and to lose,
to laugh and to grieve.
You have grace to go where you want,
to discover the outer world,
and even yourself.
There is no winning or losing,
only learning,
growing,
changing,
fulfilling what you set out to accomplish.

Forgotten

Allow the truth of who you are
to calm the trauma
of what you have experienced.
Perspective is the balm that heals the wound.
The light you have forgotten
is hidden in the center of yourself,
for it is you.
You journey through a world
of darkness,
a flesh and blood reality,
that you may discover
the parts of yourself
that you have never known.
Love and loss expand the light within.
Polarity is necessary ground,
for in it you discern yourself,
uncovering facets
that only life's experience reveals.
The memory of light returns
and sets aright the truth that fear upturned,
to lead you back to yourself,
through yourself,
beyond yourself
until the recall of all that you are
is again within your awareness.

Memory, One

What is my purpose, you asked,
when each day passes the same
and I do not progress?
The light replied,
But you do progress,
you just don't always realize it.
The world is made of indescribable light,
its fullness undisclosed to human eyes,
like the purpose of why you live.
The glory of life
is in the seeking and finding,
in the gaining and letting go,
in the magnificent and the mundane,
each moment an experience to claim.
Interpretation
is the attempt to understand purpose,
to assign meaning,
to estimate value.
But worth is not measured
by what you do or don't do,
but by who you are,
so live.
And I am always with you,
and am for you.

Reappear

The descent into shadow
to navigate unknown hues
was the experience you wanted.
This is the slow perfection—
to leave the security of light
and mine the cave of uncertainty
where darkness forms gems
you have never known.
Love.
Loss.
Joy.
Grief.
A thousand variations ebb and flow
like seasons passing one after another,
with each day bringing a new feeling,
insight,
flavor,
perspective.
The world was made for infinite potential,
the hidden game of chance and destiny.
And grasping truth is not the point,
for there is no truth here
except for what illusion represents.
Revelations of truth
are memories of light

of what you already know
but have momentarily forgotten.
You will live until you have had enough,
when all you wanted comes to completion.
And you will fade from this realm
like mist that dissipates in sunlight,
only to reappear again
in some other form,
on some other shore,
the sand and water made of golden light.

The Last of Winter

The melting snow
makes gray mist hover
through bare trees.
The sun is yet too weak to finish
what February started.
If you did not know better,
you would think this darkened light
was permanent.
But all things change.
Some things are harder than others
to accept.
Though fear at first causes trepidation,
you soon grow accustomed,
maybe even to where you can see
the beauty in the unfavorable,
in the unwanted,
or in the casualty.
But March is coming.
Winter will fade to the burgeoning of spring,
to show you what you could only imagine
from the perspective of dimmer sight.

Undercover Allies

What you remember of light
is that its golden glow
was the essence of life—
self-sustaining, loving, eternal.
You cannot see it in your passing through,
and yet you grieve it like loss.
Forgetting grants an unfamiliar stage,
that you may walk unhindered
by what you have already gained.
The hiddenness of God
is a gift you cannot acknowledge
amid the crying,
the pleading,
and the desire to understand—
the great paradox that drives your progress,
that gives you opportunity to grow.
All that is against you
is for you.
The pain you endure
and the momentary suffering
are undercover allies
in the endeavor of your soul,
to go where you have not yet gone,
to be what you have not yet become.

Worth It

You lived
despite the fear and trepidation
of a journey undisclosed in its passage,
whether it would be safe or not.
Invincible in the golden realm,
the quest to live surpassed all speculation,
uncertainty,
and the great unknown.
What will it be like?
Can I endure?
You may at times regret the fear of living,
but not when you come back home,
when the memory of light is restored.
When all is finished,
it was just a moment that passed
as fast as the twinkling of an eye,
the experience complete,
forever retained and incorporated.
Pain and sorrow are gifts you appreciate
only when you can see their purpose.
It was worth it, dear Soul, it was worth it.

Stage

The light is forever.
There is no coming and going.
Birth and death are illusions
that fool you into accepting a world of
survival,
loss,
fear,
and frustration.
You appear and disappear.
You play the part that you were meant to play.
But this life is not forever.
Only the light is forever,
the home you never leave but think you do.
Though you retain the memory of light,
it hides beneath the guise of all you see.
It is the warmth of another's arms,
the security of another's hand,
the mystery of another's eyes.
It is your own self staring back in the mirror,
wondering who you are,
where you came from,
and where you are going.

Vanished

The ache of separation
was never as strong
as when you first opened your eyes.
Fearless in the golden realm,
the memory of light
flickered and then vanished from your mind.
Such an individuation
left you with only the imagination
of oneness—
what may have been,
and what could be,
but not here.
Here, you negotiate the extremes
of darkness and light,
and every gradation in between
that experience brings.
The soul is brave to suffer for some gain,
only to be realized in the returning.
But the soul longs for union,
to eliminate the pain
of living—
the fear of survival, rejection,
and emptiness—
the lessons that it longed to navigate.

The illusion grants a false uncertainty
that only humans can know,
for only in this knowing
does purpose accomplish its task.
And the illusion will ultimately fade,
when life sees through itself,
and the knowing returns
of the life that is truly life
and was always life.

Memory, Two

Why do I suffer, you asked,
when pain is harm
against my very being?
The light replied,
The world is made in varied hues of light
to give the opportunity to see
the full potential that this life offers—
darkness and light,
fear and love,
pain and pleasure.
The spectrum of polarity
gives the potential to experience
the fulness of what can be gained,
to give knowledge of what otherwise
is impossible to understand.
The time here is momentary.
All suffering will end.
It does not mean I don't love you.
The soul is brave to descend into vulnerability
that it may ascend with the crown of wisdom.
So live.
And I am always with you,
and am for you.

Hidden

Life is a progression.
It ends the same way it begins,
with a journey from a place of safety
into the seemingly unknown.
But this unknown is not truly unknown,
only momentarily forgotten.
All you are is hidden in the soul.
Where you came from
and where you are going
play hide and seek with your curiosity.
But illusion cannot forever blur truth.
It must give way to sight,
to an uncertain knowing,
yet still a knowing.
Though you pursue understanding,
movement in unknowing leads to gain,
for the purpose is not to know fully,
but to navigate through the darkness
where hope is the wind in your sails.

Longing Light

The expectation of what you think life should be
is a dark well that never runs dry.
Surely the desire
to lessen the pain of living
gave rise to such great ideals—
reverberations of forgotten truths
that linger though you left them in the light.
And now, you can't believe what you have seen,
and how it feels.
If you could, you would remove
the evils of the world—
loss,
death,
grief,
pain,
lovelessness.
The lack of love betrays the soul within—
incoherence from its perspective.
No matter how convincing the illusion,
the light that lives within remains.
Expectation is light longing for equilibrium
of what it knows is true.
The present dimness is a purposed night
that is meant to be seen through,
for discovery and illumination.

Lost and Found

The goal was to lose yourself in the world,
to immerse yourself in a reality
so different from the light you knew
that you could no longer remember
the color of true gold.
Everything here is muted,
dimmed,
and filtered through five senses
that are geared for purposes of survival.
To be lost in the world
is to experience the world
exactly as it was made,
to have no other frame of reference
for what else might exist
outside human sight.
You wanted to live in the dark unknowing,
in the separation from your source,
in the numbness of individuality,
in the forgetting where this living comes alive,
to know the writhing of uncertainty,
the pain of abandonment,
the fear of loss,
the dissatisfaction of failure and defeat.
You wanted to have to struggle,

that you could understand
the parts of yourself
you could not know otherwise.
You wanted to search for purpose
with no chance of ever truly grasping it,
for this would ensure the inaccuracy
of your reflection in water
that never represents your true image.
The trial of human existence
is not a curse or a punishment;
it is your perfection.
There is no other meaning.

Artist

Let passion return.
Let it remind you
of what it means to live,
when all desire has faded into the background.
There was never a moment
you did not appreciate,
always showing you something
about yourself or the situation,
that it may encourage you
to move again,
to look within
that you may bring about.
You perceived the ineffable in life,
that you may express it
in the language of the soul.
Though your words are only for those
who choose to listen,
still, they shine like light
that discloses the details of the darkening—
this harshness and depth of life—
this world that exists for the discovering.

Path

The path was set, you said.
Then life brought change.
You have to walk differently now,
going where you never wanted.
The space between this reality and the ideal
is an insurmountable chasm.
Nowhere is life so dark
than in the realization of some loss,
of something your hand held
but no longer holds.
Dark and light must serve their roles—
the context of the unfolding of living.
There is no other way.
Returning is not an option.
But light never fully fades.
You may find it again
in some other form,
and its brightening will be a newness
you have not yet known here,
but, still, you will know.
You must rise and fall,
rise and fall,
until you see what you need to see
on this path of coming and going.

The Remembering

No matter how far down you go,
you must come back up.
The law of the universe
you find yourself in
prescribes the infinite potential
for all possibility.
All things have their opposite,
and every point in between.
One moment here,
one moment there,
arriving or departing,
loving or losing.
Forever you will move between the two,
that you may discover yourself
in the high and the low.
The darkness of the depth
is not permanent,
though it may feel so.
The only thing that lasts
is the light you forgot about,
that you may journey
from crest to trough to crest,
the golden shore a dream that faded upon waking,
that waits until you finally
remember.

Translucent

You will remember everything.
The moments you cherish
will not forever vanish,
though you strive to retain the feelings
of those happy times.
You replay the memories
to relive what love felt like,
though the scope through which you see
becomes translucent.
You will move forward,
for all of time moves forward.
You will not leave anything behind,
for all you experienced
is forever a part of you,
the integrated essence of your soul.
Endings are never a thing to be feared,
either yours or someone else's,
for endings are necessary—
the passing through the veil—
the return of memory
and restoration of all that happened,
all that you did,
and all who you loved.

Memory, Three

Why do I die, you asked,
when the nature of my soul
is to live?
The light replied,
Morning and evening are both beautiful,
but each in its own way.
Morning is a beginning,
the promise of what the day may bring.
Evening is the reconciliation
of all that has happened.
Each serves a purpose
in the progression of time,
of experience,
of living.
And so, death is the finality of human life,
the door that leads you back to realms of light—
the home that you forget about while here.
So, live without fear,
for I am with you
and am for you.

Quality

Why forever dwell
on the memories you cannot change?
Does replaying them
eliminate the pain?
Forcing familiarity may ease the trauma shock,
but it will not erase the history.
What is done, is done.
What is yesterday?
We look back at passed moments
from the perspective of the ongoing present.
We examine them because
they define a previous present moment—
how we behaved,
what we did,
what we said,
what we thought.
We want to comprehend the nature of the action.
We look for evidence of guilt or pardon.
We want to discern some definition of ourselves
as reflected in the action.
We want to understand ourselves.
All looking back
is an attempt to process and integrate

the forever present moments
of the stream of life,
the moments whose actions
reveal and test the quality of the soul.

Reentered

You will be okay.
What other option is there?
This is a world where torment and pain
are momentary,
illusionary,
and cannot last.
The light does not allow it
by its nature alone,
for there is only the one
that gleams in realms
outside human sight.
There is nowhere else to return to
when the last breath leaves,
carrying the soul with it
into spaces only remembered when reentered.
There was only ever one,
the one from which all things come.
Sorrow and suffering
are limited experiences
of immersion into the dim realm,
the place souls go to see,
to discover who they really are,
by forgetting who they really are,
until they return in the recovery of love.

Open

When everything feels hopeless,
when all seems meaningless,
open your eyes.
You looked all life
for what you were supposed to do,
for who you were supposed to be,
never satisfied.
What you had became the standard of success.
And what others had—
the new goal to achieve,
to prove your worth.
But value does not spring from what you do,
but from who you are.
The light in you cannot be weighed or judged;
such scrutiny is foreign to its nature.
You did not come to do,
but to be,
to experience,
to know.
Hope is based on what you do not have.
Meaning is the attempt
to make sense of the darkness.
But you are already light.
To see it,
you only have to open your eyes.

The Return of Light

Learning to lose
is not a punishment,
as if you have done something wrong.
You forget where you come from,
that you may journey unhindered
into all you are seeking.
You do not remember the golden light
and how it felt to dwell as one.
Here, you are fragmented,
scattered,
disassociated in the illusion of separation,
as if there is such a thing as other.
There was only ever union,
understanding,
completion.
The soul is brave to choose to know
what it means to shatter,
to live apart,
to suffer grief,
to be alone.
It longs to encounter fear
that it may experience darkness,
only to overcome it in the end.
All things return

from where they came.
Loss is a momentary struggle
whose purpose hides while moving through it,
only to reveal itself
in the return of light.

Now

The veil in living
is so thick and calloused
that you cannot conceive of remembering
all you have forgotten.
What was your true origin?
When did you begin?
Such questions frame the reason you are here.
You view time
as a beginning, middle, and end.
You move from present to present
creating the past and future.
But there is only now.
You cannot understand this here,
for it hides under the design of progression.
Purpose requires movement
that it may find fulfillment.
You must go from there to here,
and from here to there,
your final destination,
the journey into the succession of moments completed,
for the accumulation of experience,
for incorporation into the whole,
so that the self may know itself.

Polarity

Always seeing and dreaming of
where you want to be,
but never being there.
Such is life in the shadow of desire,
always wanting,
yearning,
striving for what you think you lack.
You cannot find the light that shines within,
for loss of memory
has darkened the doorway to enter.
You have lost your way.
But being lost is not a fault.
It is necessary polarity
so that you may find yourself again.
Light cannot hide forever.
When it returns,
it burns away the emptiness life left,
and sets you back upon the path you thought
was unrecoverable.

Memory, Four

Why do I desire, you asked,
as if my soul is never satisfied?
The light replied,
All desire stems from external stimulus
and self-judgment.
You do not know what you do not have
until you see it somewhere else.
And when you see it,
you judge yourself as lacking
that which you imagine is gain.
In the light, you are whole and complete,
with the knowing of all things.
But in the flesh, you perceive lack,
for it is gain that you are after,
for you do not remember who you are.
This is the human way—
to see and to want,
to feel and to crave,
to have and to hold,
to pursue the potential of beneficial experience
that you may understand your own reflection.
So live,
for I am with you
and am for you.

Resolute

The mistakes you made in life
must remain where you made them.
Otherwise, they will follow you
if you let them,
to remind you of who you were,
but are not anymore.
The thing you said or did
that you look back on in judgment
is a moment in time
that is gone.
It only has the power you give it.
Let it be.
You are your worst critic.
Forgiving others releases the grievances
you harbor against them,
and so does forgiving yourself.
We expect so much of ourselves
that we burn at times
in uncomfortable memories,
but this is part of being human,
learning to deal with failures
and the remorse of choices made
when hindsight shows
there were better options.

Moving forward does not require
carrying shame or regret,
but only the acceptance of
what you cannot go back and change.

Pinnacle

Fear is the pinnacle of the illusion
that all lifelong you fight.
But shadows are for walking through,
not for remaining in.
How else would you come to know yourself,
if nothing ever pushed or stressed your soul?
This life is for facing the struggle,
the hardship,
the challenge you desired
but now cannot remember.
It is better this way.
This is the time where you move,
where you grow when you falter
but get up again,
where you change when you realize
you could have done better,
where you navigate the limits of the self
and how far you can stretch.
You will not be disappointed in the end.
You left yourself
to find yourself again,
that you may become golden.

Navigate

Past the edge of what you can endure,
the light is a barely perceptible dimness,
an afterthought of what you hoped would be,
like traveling and then
forgetting where you began,
or where you are going.
It is not that the light is cruel
to hide itself from you;
it is allowing you
to fulfill the reason you are here,
and all you came to do.
The brave soul longs to navigate its bounds
while descended and veiled in flesh,
the acquired blindness of living,
that it may see past itself
in the expansion of understanding,
of everything that is possible.
You are not forsaken,
although it may feel so.
There is only a moving forward,
finalizing in an ultimate remembering
and incorporation of discovery.

Moon

Desire is never satisfied,
even in the getting
and the holding.
The heart can never rest
in what it has received,
because the purpose of life is not to have,
but to experience;
human nature does not realize this,
for it only yearns and grasps
to ensure its own survival.
Newness and excitement wane,
like the moon that loses its light
when it has had enough of fullness.
It must return to emptiness
so that it can grow in desire again,
for it is the seeking that it is after,
the process of enlightenment
to illuminate its inner being,
the true light that never fades.

Rhythms

Asleep in the rhythms of life,
destiny and purpose pave the path
to move you from one thing to another,
through the good and the bad,
through the desired and the feared—
the life you chose but can't remember why.
Repetition masks the deeper self.
But this will not last forever.
You will awaken and renew
when you have had enough of the forgetting—
of living blindly through
the rise and fall of emotion,
the yearning for fulfillment,
the pursual that longing births,
the weariness expectations bring.
The question *why* is light that can't push through.
The veil you wear allows your soul to learn.
You must ascend.
You must rush up
like from the depth of a dream,
where you open your eyes and awareness returns,
a new birth,
a resurrection,
a remembering of who you are,
of all you are.

Persist

To continue through failure
takes courage to see beyond
what the pain reinforces—
hopelessness ingrained in memory.
Effort put forth,
message received.
Results can paralyze the will,
or strengthen it to take another step.
Always the challenge of intention and obstacle,
in a world designed to maximize
some forward movement of light,
whose purpose is your gain.
Energy out,
experience received.
Faltering unveils the need within,
the necessary darkness
that illuminates the potential of growth,
that you may get up and try again.

Pierce

Fear returned
when you saw a similar pattern emerge.
You've been through this before.
So it's back to anticipating moments
you don't want to experience,
hypervigilant in your vision
of how the road curves and bends ahead.
The distance veils the outcome.
The unknown causes trepidation.
Past hurt fuels anxiety.
But you don't have to suffer
under the fear of self-preservation,
of how human nature responds instinctually
to survive at any cost,
with warning signs that echo through the body.
Life in the forgetting
is a constant struggle
of observation and understanding,
of looking for light to lead your way,
of coming up from some inner depth,
until you pierce the firmament
to see that what you thought was true
was just a fragment of a higher truth.

Memory, Five

Why does fear exist, you asked,
when the heart only wants to love?
The light replied,
Fear can only dwell in light so dim
that you cannot see your way.
It is a by-product of a world
created to harbor polarity,
where objects can block light and form shadows.
You cannot remember the realm of light
while walking in the flesh.
The human is forsaken to its role—
to yearn for understanding,
to hope in lack of proof,
to struggle to survive.
The intention to know yourself differently
accepts an illusive state of oblivion,
to immerse into the unknown of the potential.
So live, learn, grow, change,
for I am with you
and am for you.

Expand

When you awaken,
it is not the world that has changed,
but yourself.
You first subject yourself to dimmer light
in the hope that in its obscurity
you may find some new perspective,
revealing some new aspect of the soul.
The moments in amnesia mean the most—
actions in the context of the unknowing
that test the baseline absent of the light.
But illusions can't forever hold their guise,
for their very nature is to conceal
what otherwise can never be unmade.
All of life is a progression,
a slow unveiling
whose inevitable destiny
is expanded awareness
in the fullness of remembrance.

Liberation

You desired liberation from the pain
but did not know how to reach it.
So, you suffered through
days and nights
at the mercy of uncontrollable thoughts—
Why? and *When will this end?*
Giving up was not an option.
No one waited for your surrender.
Sometimes the prison is self-imposed,
with the key hidden in your pocket.
Inner turmoil can block rationality,
capturing you in its grip.
Breathe—
peace can return in the midst of confusion,
even absent of the answer.
Refocus—
the light never fully disappears
and is stronger than the shadows.
Be still—
patience gives the forward path
time to appear,
that you may see it and walk.

Flight

You wanted to leave everything behind
and run away.
But this is not freedom.
The demands and responsibilities of life
triggered the instinct to survive,
similar to the threat of death.
Running was the promise of self-preservation
amid the oppression of the
have-to, the *must*, and the *or else*.
But this is not living.
It is okay to ask for help,
to reevaluate where you are
and what you are doing.
You can find hope
in the strength of resistance,
in learning to do
what feels impossible,
in going where you have never gone,
in becoming what you never thought you could.

The Recovery of Light

Only in the forgetting
do souls harm one another.
The veil
and the instinctual human animal
give occasion for such trauma,
all in the name of the threat of
physical survival.
The beautiful and the terrible are built in
to the forgetting,
laid out before you like a game board
on which you chose to move,
where terror and glory weigh on the scales,
and a timer ever ticks down.
You will interpret this
as something you must somehow win,
but only the illusion of winning exists here;
competition is a system feature.
Hidden away, the light in you
wants love to rule the world,
but darkness is intentional dissonance,
the cause for the ultimate question, *Why?*
Once ascended from the forgetting,
you will judge yourself
against all you now remember—

who you are and all you are—
in all you did and why.
You will process and understand,
examine every angle,
and incorporate all experience
in the recovery of light.

Pursuit

There is time here to capture
everything you wanted,
to see to its end
all you hoped for,
to experience in totality
all you desired.
Opportunity will come and go.
Life here is both vibrant and robust,
and brittle and frail;
each will serve you
in the discovery of purpose and meaning,
but neither will give away the answer.
Though destiny will present
in one form or another
the chance for fulfillment
of all you set out to do,
whether you grasp it or not
is not the point;
reaching holds more value than obtaining,
disclosing the worth of what could be.

Differences

You have fought it long enough.
Now is the time for acceptance
of what you cannot change.
Allowing what is out of your control
does not mean you approve.
It does not mean you condone
what you disagree with.
Emotions may flood you with
the desire to disassociate,
or to attack another as an enemy.
But life is not for getting others to agree with you,
but for loving them even amid the differences.
Life hits each soul with trial and turmoil,
with confusion and uncertainty,
with pressure of what to do next,
with what to believe or think,
with the whole world's existence seemingly at stake.
Love is greater than the sum of opinion or preference.
Love does not project its fears
or insecurities on another,
as if to satisfy some inner need.
Love is the light that holds another
even in the dimness of uncertainty.

Collective

Human nature desires independence,
to walk its own path
regardless of the burden it carries.
It wants to do for itself
and not to have to need another.
Survival is the primal fear,
convincing you that needfulness is weakness,
and weakness is the harbinger of death.
But you are here to know the limitation
of what it means to be human,
to navigate the bounds of life and death,
to grow under the veil of mortality,
to learn to overcome
what you thought was impossible.
You are not alone.
You can try to bear the weight on your own,
or you can ask for help.
No shame exists in asking,
only the strength of the collective,
the hint of union
in some sacred space you cannot quite remember,
but feel in another's hand.

Memory, Six

Why must I grieve, you asked,
when those who I love leave?
The light replied,
The leaving is the hardest for the human,
the loss of what you loved about another.
Does loss exist absent of love?
So, love creates the bond between the two,
but severs from the vantage of the flesh.
Grief is in the severance,
the perceived experience of loss,
in the no longer, the no more,
and the now what?
Loss feels permanent
in a world where nothing is permanent,
the human only knowing what it sees.
Grief brings about acceptance of change,
of moving forward with remembrance,
a salve to help the wound heal,
and the expectation of what it means
to stand again anew on the golden shore,
the destiny of all who walk the earth.
So live and love fully,
for I am with you
and am for you.

Blur

Enough years have passed
where you no longer remember your youth—
what you did from day to day,
the games you played,
the places you went,
the long summers.
Such is the passage of time,
the string of moments
that create your reality,
with each day pushing
past days farther away,
until they blur into the background.
But this is what has made you who you are.
Each day is a chance to
learn and grow,
seek and find,
or let go.
All things work for your gain,
whether you realize it or not.
You do not have to like it.
You only need to live.

Uplift

It is hard to see the positive
when mired in the negative—
the abandonment of light
in a world that allows darkness
as necessary polarity.
Darkness is not forever—
you know this—
although it does not feel so.
The bleak uncertainty
and the threat of fear
are overwhelming,
paralyzing,
and block the light you know must still exist.
The nature of light is to uplift,
to bring remembrance of what is good,
to infuse the heart with the will to live,
to continue,
to push through what seems impenetrable,
to stand again with the intention to move,
to walk again with strength and certainty,
to see again the beauty of the unfolded flower,
the bee dusted with pollen,
the butterfly wing.

Rising

Rise again.
Awaken from your slumber.
The world may burden you
with sadness and sorrow,
but you do not have to
hold its dim light.
Growth has taught you how to let it go.
So, release it.
Let it slip from your grasp
with the same certainty you had
when you first received it,
not knowing what was happening
or how to handle it.
Though you never asked for it,
the hard road of experience
brought you to a higher place,
where you can look back and see
the obstacles you got through.
Nothing is impossible for you
except for what you otherwise accept.
Even in the midst of struggle,
illumination reveals itself
in the letting go and the rising.

Clarity

Do not despair.
The end is never final,
no matter how bad it feels.
Continuation is the nature of the thing,
into places you cannot see or imagine
from your single perspective.
You must grieve
so that you may understand,
for the one who experiences all knows all.
And the knowing provides clarity,
even of what your human eyes cannot see.
It is the only path to peace,
which allows acceptance,
and the ability to move on.
You are not alone.
All who have gone before you understand.
It is yours to discover,
to uncover,
to wrestle with and see through,
until what is unknown reveals itself
and illuminates the soul.

Looking

The nature of the world is dim enough
to give you opportunity to see
the deepest part of yourself.
The soul contrasts against this darker light.
You are better for the journey,
though it may not seem so
in the passing through.
Perfection comes from trying again,
not from getting it all right the first time.
Learning is what the soul wants,
for it longs to know itself
amid the terror and the treasure,
the horror and the happiness.
The soul is brave to look into itself,
for this is the finding out,
the perceiving,
the knowing,
the reason for such a descent
in the purpose of living.

Emergence

Grief is like dark woods
you cannot see through
until you are in them.
From the outside,
it is a dense, bleak unknowing.
Fear causes hesitation—
you do not want to go inside
in case the darkness may be permanent,
or you cannot find your way.
But still, you must choose to enter.
Once in, your eyes adjust.
You can distinguish trees, leaves, ground cover,
and the scant path others found before you.
There is no going back,
but only moving forward.
Each careful step
is a sliver of hope,
a different understanding,
a processing of feeling and emotion,
a reconciliation of life and loss.
Acceptance is the light that peeks through trees,
signaling the edge is near,
the emergence from this depth,
this journey to recover,
this unexpected renewal.

Extend

Be light.
Forever shine,
so that others may see in the dark.
Why hold in
what can help others,
whether they acknowledge it or not?
Another's response of gratitude
or lack of appreciation
does not dictate
whether you extend or retract your hand.
The soul grows most when it gives,
for it is in putting others first
that it learns its true potential—
to be life when the will flickers,
to be strength when there is none,
to be love in the worry of abandonment.
Light looks into the darkness
that it may illuminate the dim spaces
where souls struggle and wane,
to help them stand,
to help them heal.

Rediscovery

Choose to love,
whether you want to or not.
The world is dark despite the light within
that hides beneath the human condition—
survival at any cost.
The fear of death is a veil that blinds the heart
from realizing its potential,
if it could only overcome its bounds.
And this is the opportunity
you were looking for—
to struggle within the polarity of
life and death,
of breath and body,
that you may come to understand
the harmful and the helpful,
the setback and the breakthrough,
the surrender and the triumph.
Love is the light that shows the way
through whatever would impede you.
Love is your true nature,
the guide on the journey
of finding yourself again.

Memory, Seven

Why do I struggle to love, you asked,
when I know love is the way?
The light replied,
When the soul enters flesh,
its expression dims
through what the body allows—
like light diffused in translucence,
obscuring pure clarity.
Fear of survival,
instinctual desire,
and physical limitations
all oppose the light that lives within.
The soul must learn to navigate constraint,
to leap the chasm of natural limitation,
to overcome the barrier of the human self—
the insistence that its needs come first,
regardless of the cost.
Love betrays the instinct to survive,
and stabs it in its relentless, selfish heart,
so that the shedding of blood purifies the soul
to give it chance to live as it intends.

Hollow

This loss was a strike to the heart
whose pain was a hollowing out
of the good in the world.
Absence felt like soul sickness
with no foreseeable cure.
So you slept and woke up,
slept and woke up,
until time brought you forward enough
so you could breathe again.
Time—
the foe and friend of life—
ticking down and taking away,
then moving forward to foster healing.
Perspective changes with the passage of moments.
Processing allows thought and emotion
to be seen and heard,
to state their grievances,
to swell and subside.
Everything returns in the end.
There is no true loss,
only the momentary experience of it.
The soul remembers the good in another,
love that not even death can take away.

Woven

Be happy making others happy.
What greater purpose
is there in living?
When you spend your life
trying to get all you desire,
you eventually see its futility.
The one who helps others is more fulfilled
than he who only helps himself.
All lifelong you search for meaning,
not realizing you find it
in how you give of yourself.
The love of self is woven in the flesh;
the love of others, in the soul.

Without

You move through the world
in the full awareness of its potential,
that you cannot control life's endings.
This is the risk of living.
What is known is hard to lose,
for it is the shared experiences
that create the union.
The severing leaves a void
that no one can cross.
But even this has a purpose.
Letting go does not mean forsaking love.
For though you cannot reach the golden realm,
love does—
the bond that death cannot unbind or break.
Love lives on in the memory of another.

Endurance

You wanted to escape life
and the continual responsibilities
that present themselves as challenges.
They burdened you upon waking,
flooding in as remembrances
of the new day's difficulties.
It never ends, you said.
Sleep was a forgetting—
a momentary excursion
through dreams of foreign lands
and interactions with people,
some now gone and some still here—
the pleasure and relief of a different life
with no place for anxiety or worry,
but only journey and discovery.
But the morning brought you back,
your first thoughts the burn
of the burdens of the day.
I cannot do this anymore, you said.
But you can, the light replied.
You will get through today
just as you got through yesterday,
and all the days before.
This season will not last forever,

though some seasons are harder than others.
Although it may not seem so,
all is working for your gain.
Each day builds to something better,
something to look forward to,
that makes this life worthwhile.
The end of summer brings the changing leaves,
the end of winter brings the budding flower.

Complete

To understand yourself
from the perspective of dimmer light,
this world provides the opportunity
to seek the depth that you have never known.
Happiness and sadness come and go;
they balance the restlessness within
that knows time is limited.
This journey has an ending.
Nothing here is meant to last,
but to be experienced
with all it has to offer.
Polarity gives chance for both extremes
and everything in between.
One is not better than the other,
if your perspective is to know yourself
in what love and loss feel like.
Highs and lows test the soul
to reveal the path that brings you to completion.

Aftermath

Life continues, even in hardship.
Regardless of the severity,
you will pass through.
Struggles and drama are momentary
in the long strand of life.
The disaster you fear
may never come,
but if it does,
it too will pass.
You do not have to understand its purpose,
or lose yourself in the why.
With living comes the endless potential
for every sort of experience.
Learning to handle the negative
is a lesson life teaches
in the brunt of the aftermath.
But this is how you grow.

Memory, Leaves

"Today grieves, tomorrow grieves,
Cover me over light in leaves."
-T.S. Eliot

Watching the leaves fall in Ohio,
I rest against the dry earth of autumn
and bury my arms in layers of leaves.

I imagine the places I could be,
knowing the rush and scuttle of autumn,
my legs buried in layers of leaves:

I remember my brother in orange October,
green sweatshirt, jeans, and dirty sneakers,
burying himself in layers of leaves;

the dog in the yard is barking at flashes
of reds and yellows falling from trees,
his paws are buried in layers of leaves;

the neighbors are out gathering leaves,
raking along the dry earth of autumn
all shapes and colors in layers of leaves;

my mother calls me in for dinner,
she cannot see me buried in leaves,
resting against the dry earth of autumn.

Experience

It's only for a moment that we live,
going here and there,
doing this and that,
all the while trying to understand
our purpose and place in the world.
We lose ourselves in living
so that we can feel the depth
of new uncertainties,
not knowing what will come,
or with what degree of emotion.
We forget our place of origin
so that we can find ourselves anew
on foreign shores,
the playing field of fantasy and dream.
Experience is gold in varied form,
the desire of the soul to see itself,
to test itself,
to know itself,
to find light again.

The Memory of Light

You will move
in the silent numbness of the forgetting
until the golden light illuminates your soul,
revealing what you never expected
or could have imagined
from the perspective of fragmentation.
You drifted down
until you no longer recognized yourself
or your true home.
Even the excitement you had in starting
was lost in the descent.
Upon arrival, everything was new again.
Though the light was dimmer,
all notions of origin
vanished from recollection.
The first breath was the dawn of life.
You became one of them,
living and moving in limited flesh.
Mortality was the primeval fear,
whose goal was the perfection of the soul.
The formation of desire
and its satisfaction
were the outworking of human survival—
loss and gain,

need and abundance,
pain and pleasure,
the measure of experience and possibility.
The design was the immersion in a reality
that required ignorance of anything outside it,
beyond it,
invisible to human eyes.
Emotion grounded you in the body,
your response to the natural environment—
fear, hunger, longing, isolation—
the necessary pressure of endeavor,
the fear of death the primal catalyst.
Logic grounded your discernment,
the governing faculty for understanding the world—
imagination, rationality, deduction, conclusion.
The goodness in life
blurred the boundary of purpose beyond survival,
provoking thoughts that something more exists
than what the eyes see
or the hands touch,
though never able to provide conclusive proof.
Illusion does not give itself away.
The dreamer does not know he is dreaming,
until he awakens to reflect on
where he seemingly has been.
The light was a foreign concept
upon hearing about it for the first time,
a hope born from desperation
of the human condition,

of the struggle to live,
to survive,
to love.
The nature of the soul is peace,
for it bears the image of its source
from which its existence derives.
It seeks the equilibrium of love,
for the center of its being
is inclined to resonate
with the oneness it has now forgotten.
The pressure of flesh disturbs its essence,
overshadowing its capacity,
demanding to be put first,
to be satisfied, to be fed.
The light was an answer to the fear of
loneliness, frailty, fault, and guilt—
struggles that caused the soul to look within,
to look without,
to question the way and the why of the world.
Desperation fuels discovery,
instigated from necessity.
But it was the touch of another's hand
that brought forth the feeling of union,
a memory of light triggered
in the dimness of the forgetting,
a partial recollection of the oneness
retained within the illusion,
because the essence of the one
cannot be completely veiled.

Light by nature never yields to darkness,
but only can disguise itself
as dimmer light.
All lifelong you fought to know the truth,
of who you are
and where you came from.
Love and darkness share a boundary
that never fully dissolves,
regardless of the golden light you see.
This is not a mistake,
but fulfillment of the purpose of living.
Light divine is hidden by design.
It also remains within,
for it is life.
Ultimately, this journey will end,
as all journeys end,
and the time to return will come,
the golden shore again within your view,
regardless of what you were able to see,
or what you believed.
Love is what matters most—
the essence of the light that shines forever.
The light will say,
Return to me,
to the full recollection of who you are,
of all you are,
of all you have done and become.
The glory of the soul
unveils in the memory of light.

Thematic Subject Index

The poems in this book contain a variety of themes. Sometimes, a single poem will touch on multiple themes. The following subject index lists out some of the more major themes and highlights where they are more prominently featured.

About the Author

Keith Wrassmann holds the degrees of MA in Creative Writing: Poetry from Miami University (Oxford, OH) and MDiv in Theology from Cincinnati Christian University, where he also won the Theological Studies Award. He lives in the greater Cincinnati, Ohio area with his wife and children.

Visit www.keithwrassmann.com for more.

www.ingramcontent.com/pod-product-compliance
Lightning Source LLC
LaVergne TN
LVHW050937080826
845145LV00004B/1299

* 9 7 8 1 9 6 1 6 3 1 0 5 2 *